Contents

MY NLP MANUAL

A BEGINNER'S HANDBOOK TO SUCCESS

SMRUTHI RAAGVNDRA

INDIA • SINGAPORE • MALAYSIA

ISBN 979-8-89067-904-8

Introduction

Once upon a time, there was a person called Sid who always had a negative mindset. He would tell himself that he was not good enough, he would fail, and people would judge him. These thoughts had been with him for so long that they had become a part of him, and he couldn't see a way to change himself.

One day, Sid met a neuro-linguistic programming (NLP) practitioner, who showed him how to use the power of language to change his inner dialogue. The practitioner used a metaphor to explain how language can impact our thoughts and behaviors.

The practitioner said, "Imagine you're hiking in the woods, and you come across a sign that says 'Dangerous path ahead. Stay away.' You would probably avoid that path because the language on the sign makes you feel fearful and unsure. But imagine if the sign said, 'Exciting path ahead. Explore with caution.' This language makes you feel curious and adventurous, and you would be more likely to take that path."

Sid realized that the words he used to describe himself were like the sign in the woods. If he used negative language, he would feel negative emotions, and his behavior would match that. But if he used positive language and reframed his thoughts, he could change his emotions and behavior.

Using NLP techniques, Sid learned to change his inner dialogue. He started telling himself that he was capable, successful, and loved. Over time, his negative mindset faded away, and he became a confident and positive person.

The moral of the story is that the language we use can impact our thoughts and behaviors. By using NLP techniques, we can change our inner dialogue and create a positive impact on our lives.

Neuro-linguistic programming (NLP) coaching is a powerful and effective method of coaching that is focused on helping individuals achieve personal and professional success by developing their communication and behavioral skills. Here are some of the benefits of NLP coaching:

1. **Improved communication skills:** NLP coaching helps individuals improve their communication skills by teaching them how to express their thoughts and ideas clearly and effectively. This can lead to better relationships, greater influence and increased success in personal and professional life.

2. **Increased self-awareness:** NLP coaching helps individuals to become more self-aware by identifying their strengths, weaknesses, beliefs and values. This awareness can help them to make informed decisions, set realistic goals and take actions that are aligned with their personal and professional values.

3. **Enhanced problem-solving skills:** NLP coaching teaches people how to approach problems and challenges in a more structured and strategic way. This can lead to better decision-making and a more positive outlook on life.

4. **Improved emotional intelligence:** NLP coaching helps individuals to develop their emotional intelligence by teaching them how to identify and manage their emotions. This can lead to greater self-awareness, better relationships, and improved resilience in the face of challenges.

5. **Increased confidence and motivation:** NLP coaching can help individuals to build their self-confidence and motivation by teaching them effective techniques for overcoming limiting beliefs and negative self-talk. This can lead to increased success in all areas of life.

Overall, NLP coaching offers a range of benefits for individuals who want to achieve personal and professional success. It can help individuals to develop their communication skills, increase their self-awareness, enhance their problem-solving skills, improve their emotional intelligence, and build their confidence and motivation.

Neuro-Linguistic Programming or NLP is a technique that has been used for decades and is an effective way to improve communication, change behaviors and overcome negative patterns. NLP is a combination of psychology, linguistics, and neuroscience that aims to help individuals achieve their desired goals through effective communication and personal development.

This book is all about introducing a novice to Neuro linguistic programming, the concept of the mind, and how it works. The book will explore the basics of NLP and its applications and help the reader understand how to use NLP in their everyday lives.

Chapter 1: What is NLP?

In this chapter, the book will provide an overview of NLP and define it in simplest terms. It will discuss the origin, history, and the pioneers of NLP. It will also provide an overview of the NLP model, its principles, philosophy, and how it can be used to improve communication, behavior, and performance.

Chapter 2: Understanding the Mind

This chapter will delve deep into the concept of the mind and its workings. It will explain the conscious and the unconscious mind, their roles in shaping thoughts, emotions, and behaviors. The chapter will clarify the role of the mind in response to stimuli, and the power of thoughts to influence behaviors.

Chapter 3: NLP Techniques

In this chapter, readers will explore key NLP techniques that they can use to improve their communication skills, build rapport, and model the behavior of successful individuals. Techniques like anchoring, reframing, and rapport building will be explained in easy-to-understand language.

Chapter 4: Applications of NLP

The fourth chapter of the book will explore the different areas where NLP can be applied. From personal development and self-confidence to business communication and therapy, the chapter will present real-life examples of how NLP has been used to help individuals achieve their goals.

Chapter 5: Conclusion

In the final chapter, the book will summarize the key concepts of NLP and provide a roadmap for beginners to continue their NLP journey. The book will recommend additional resources, workshops, and courses to help readers deepen their understanding of NLP.

Chapter 1

What is NLP?

NLP (Neuro-Linguistic Programming) is an approach to personal and professional development. It was created in the 1970s by John Grinder, a linguist, and Richard Bandler, a computer scientist, and mathematician. NLP is based on the concept that the mind, language, and behavior are interrelated and can be programmed to achieve specific goals or outcomes.

The origins of NLP can be traced back to the work of psychologists Milton Erickson, Virginia Satir, and Fritz Perls, who were known for their techniques in psychotherapy. Grinder and Bandler studied the work of these experts and developed techniques for modeling their behaviors and language patterns.

The term "Neuro-Linguistic Programming" was coined by Bandler and Grinder in the early 1970s. They began teaching NLP to others through workshops and became known as the pioneers of NLP. They published their first book, "The Structure of Magic," in 1975, and later released other books on NLP, such as "Frogs into Princes" and "Refining the Art of Modeling."

Over the years, NLP has evolved and developed into different branches, such as NLP coaching, NLP therapy, and NLP business. Today, NLP is widely used in various fields, such as business, leadership, education, sports, and personal development.

Today, many experts in NLP continue to expand on the work of Grinder and Bandler, such as Robert Dilts, Judith DeLozier, Steve Andreas, and many others. Although NLP has had some controversy and criticism over the years, it remains a popular approach for personal and professional development, and has helped many people achieve their goals and overcome challenges in their lives.

Neuro-Linguistic Programming is a powerful technique that can help individuals improve their communication, change behaviors, and achieve their goals. This book has been written for beginners to introduce them to the basics of NLP and its applications in everyday life. By the end of the book, the reader will have a clear understanding of the NLP model, the workings of the mind, and a set of powerful techniques to use in their personal and professional lives.

Neuro-Linguistic Programming (NLP) uses a variety of techniques to help individuals train both their conscious and unconscious mind. NLP techniques can be used to strengthen positive behaviors and eliminate negative ones. The following are some techniques that can help with conscious and unconscious training:

1. Conscious Training

- **Self-Talk:** Self-talk is the practice of speaking positive affirmations to oneself. It can be used to change negative self-talk to positive self-talk. Positive messages can be repeated to oneself like "I am confident and capable", "I am successful in all areas of my life," etc.

NLP can help take unwanted, negative self-talk and turn it into positive self-talk, which can change a person's attitude and boost self-confidence.

- **Goal Setting:** Setting achievable goals using SMART (Specific, Measurable, Achievable, Relevant, and Time-bound) principles is a powerful technique that can be used with NLP to achieve conscious results. This not only helps individuals focus on their desired outcomes but also enables them to identify and work towards their goals more effectively.

2. Unconscious Training

- **Visualization:** Visualization is a technique that uses positive mental imagery to help individuals achieve their desired outcomes. It can be used to change negative images associated with past events and memories that may be preventing an individual from achieving their desired outcomes. Visualization can be used to create new beliefs, behaviors, and habits by imagining them in the mind's eye.

- **Anchoring:** Anchoring is a technique that helps individuals to create positive feelings, emotions or behaviors and then anchor them in place. This can be done by associating the positive feeling attached to a physical sensation such as a hand gesture to help retrieve the positive emotions or behaviors later, as required.

- **Reframing:** Reframing helps change negative or limiting beliefs by changing the context in which they are presented. The objective is to take a limiting belief and put it into a more positive light, thus shifting its focus towards a more desirable outcome.

By training both the conscious and unconscious mind, NLP can help individuals create positive changes and shift behaviors from negative to positive. They can acquire the tools to improve communication, emotions, and behaviors that allow them to achieve personal and professional success.

Chapter 2

Understanding the mind!

Neuro-Linguistic Programming (NLP) is a technique that helps individuals to understand the mind, language, and behavior more effectively. It uses a variety of techniques to help individuals identify problematic behaviors and beliefs and replace them with positive alternatives that lead to personal and professional growth and success. Here are a few ways in which NLP helps individuals understand their mind:

1. Mind-Body Connection

The mind-body connection is like a bridge between the conscious and unconscious mind. It's like a river that flows between physical sensation and emotional experience. Just as a bridge connects two points, the mind and body are interconnected, and NLP is the tool that helps us understand and improve this connection. It's like the cable that connects the bridge and helps it to support weight, or in this case, our thoughts and emotions. NLP helps us rewire our thought patterns, allowing us to translate our thoughts and emotions into physical sensations and actions. By improving the mind-body connection through NLP, we can create a healthier, more balanced life.

There once was a young woman named Priya who had always struggled with her weight. She felt constantly hungry and out of control around food, often binge eating late at night when no one was watching. She disliked her body and felt uncomfortable in her own skin.

One day, Priya heard about Neuro Linguistic Programming and decided to give it a try. She started practicing NLP techniques to reprogram her thoughts and beliefs about food, exercise, and her body. She learned to listen to her body and understand its signals. Slowly but surely, she began to feel more in control, more confident, and more at peace with herself.

As she continued to practice NLP, Priya started to notice a change in her physical body as well. She had more energy, slept better, and felt more motivated to exercise. She stopped binge eating and started to make healthier choices that felt good to her body. Before she knew it, the weight she had struggled with for years had started to come off naturally and sustainably.

Priya realized that her mind and body were deeply connected, and by shifting her mindset, she was able to transform her physical body as well. From that moment on, she continued to practice NLP and nourish her mind and body with healthy habits. She felt more confident, happy, and balanced in all areas of her life, and she knew that the mind-body connection was the key to her success.

NLP emphasizes the importance of the connection between the mind and body. It helps individuals to understand how thoughts, emotions, and beliefs are interconnected and can affect physical sensations and responses. This awareness can help an individual learn to manage their emotional state more effectively, thus relieving physical and emotional stress.

The mind-body connection is a key aspect of Neuro-linguistic programming (NLP). NLP focuses on the ways in which our thoughts, language, and behavior impact our physical and emotional health. Here are some ways that NLP can be used to enhance the mind body connection:

- **Managing stress:** NLP techniques can be used to manage stress, which can have a negative impact on both physical and mental health. Techniques such as reframing negative beliefs and using visualization can help individuals to manage stress and promote relaxation.

- **Enhancing physical performance:** By using NLP techniques to visualize and set achievable goals, individuals can enhance their athletic performance and abilities.

- **Reducing pain:** NLP techniques can be used to reduce pain levels by teaching individuals how to control their thoughts and emotions in response to pain.

- **Promoting healing:** NLP techniques can be used to promote healing by reducing stress and promoting positive thinking. This can enhance physical healing and improve overall health and well-being.

- **Improving self-awareness:** By using NLP techniques to reflect on thoughts, emotions, and behaviors, individuals can improve their self-awareness and better understand the relationship between their mental and physical health.

Overall, NLP can be a valuable tool for enhancing the mind-body connection, promoting stress management, improving physical performance and reducing pain, promoting healing, and improving self-awareness.

2. Perception

NLP helps individuals understand how internal factors such as beliefs, values, and attitudes influence their perception of the world around them. It teaches individuals to shift the focus from negative thoughts to positive ones, creating a more optimistic outlook to life.

Rani was a young, enthusiastic marketer who was looking forward to landing her dream job at a top advertising agency in town. She was confident in her abilities and had all the necessary qualifications to excel in the role.

But on the day of her job interview, Rani found herself facing a panel of six stern-faced executives who seemed to be scrutinizing her every move. Despite her best efforts, she stumbled through the interview and left feeling defeated.

As she replayed the events of the day in her mind, Rani realized that she had made a critical mistake. In her nervousness, she had assumed that the panel of executives was judging her performance and questioning her abilities. But upon reflection, she realized that this was just her perception of the situation. In reality, the executives were simply trying to get a sense of her personality, work ethic, and communication skills.

Determined to turn things around, Rani began to employ techniques from Neuro Linguistic Programming which she had come across recently. By shifting her perception of the situation, she was able to reframe the interview as an opportunity to showcase her strengths and abilities rather than a judgment of her inadequacies.

Over the following weeks, Rani undertook an intensive NLP training program that helped her to identify and control her automatic thought patterns. She also learned how to use language more effectively to influence her own behavior and the behavior of others.

By the time the next job interview rolled around, Rani was a new person altogether. She exuded confidence, composure, and charisma, all of which were evident to the panel of executives. She aced the interview and was promptly offered the job.

Rani's story is a powerful testament to the power of perception and the benefits of Neuro Linguistic Programming. By changing her perception of a situation, she was able to transform her reality and achieve the success that she had always dreamed of.

Perception refers to the way in which we interpret and make sense of sensory information from our environment. It involves the processing of incoming signals through our senses such as sight, sound, touch, taste, and smell, which are then translated into meaningful experiences.

NLP, on the other hand, is a psychological approach that was developed in the 1970s which focuses on the language, thoughts, and behaviors that we use to create our reality. It involves the study of the ways in which we use language to represent our experiences and how we can use this knowledge to facilitate positive change.

The relationship between perception and NLP lies in the fact that our perception influences the way we process and interpret language. For example, our beliefs, values, emotions, and past experiences affect the way we understand and respond to the language used by others and ourselves. NLP techniques can be used to change the way we perceive and interpret language, leading to improved communication and personal growth. Similarly, NLP can also be used to change our perception of our environment, leading to more positive and . empowering experiences.

3. Communication

NLP emphasizes the importance of effective communication, both with oneself and with others. It helps individuals understand how language, tone, and nonverbal cues can affect communication and how to overcome barriers to effective communication such as stereotypes, biases, and assumptions.

Dia had always struggled with public speaking. Every time she had to give a presentation or talk in front of a crowd, she would freeze up, forget her points, and stumble over her words. It was frustrating and embarrassing, especially since she knew she was knowledgeable and capable.

One day, Dia decided she had had enough and sought out a Neuro linguistic programming (NLP) coach. The coach taught her about the power of internal dialogue and external communication, and how they could be used to improve her public speaking skills.

Dia learned that her internal dialogue, or the conversations she had with herself in her head, played a huge role in how she presented herself externally. If she constantly told herself that she was a terrible public speaker and that she would mess up, her body would respond to that negative self-talk, causing her to feel anxious and nervous.

To combat this, Dia practiced positive self-talk before every speaking engagement. She reminded herself that she was knowledgeable, prepared, and confident. She visualized herself giving a successful presentation and receiving praise and recognition afterwards. By doing this, her body responded positively, and she felt more relaxed and in control.

Externally, Dia learned how to communicate effectively with her audience. She worked on her posture, making sure she stood tall with her shoulders back, and made eye contact with everyone in the room. She practiced using NLP techniques such as pacing and leading, where she would mirror the body language and tone of her audience before gradually leading them towards a more positive and persuasive message.

The more Dia practiced these techniques, the more confident she became in her public speaking abilities. She impressed her colleagues with her informative and engaging presentations, and even landed a promotion at work because of her newfound skills.

In the end, Dia realized that the key to success was not just about what she said, but also about how she said it. By using NLP to improve her internal dialogue and external communication, she was able to overcome her fear of public speaking and achieve her goals.

4. Belief System

NLP encourages individuals to recognize and challenge their limiting beliefs and values. It helps to increase the level of self-awareness and recognize any negative patterns of thinking that may prevent them from achieving their desired goals.

Adarsh had always believed that he wasn't good enough. He grew up in a family where academic achievement was highly valued, but no matter how hard he tried, he never felt like he measured up. As an adult, this belief followed him into his professional and personal life, causing him to doubt himself and miss out on opportunities.

One day, Adarsh decided he had enough and sought out a Neuro-linguistic programming (NLP) coach. The coach taught him that beliefs are just thoughts that we have repeated over and over again, and that they can be changed with practice and intention.

Adarsh learned to identify his limiting beliefs and examine the evidence that supported them. He realized that just because he had struggled academically in the past, it didn't mean he was incapable of learning or growing. The coach helped him reframe his negative beliefs into more positive and empowering ones, such as "I am capable of learning and improving every day."

Adarsh also practiced visualization techniques, where he imagined himself doing well and achieving his goals. This helped him to feel more confident and motivated, and he started to notice positive changes in his life. He took on new challenges at work and in his personal life, and found that he was achieving more than he ever thought possible.

Over time, Adarsh's belief in himself grew stronger and stronger. He no longer felt held back by his past failures, and instead focused on the present moment and what he could do to improve. He even took on a leadership role at work, which he previously thought was impossible for him.

Adarsh's transformation showed him the power of belief change with NLP. He learned that our thoughts and beliefs shape our reality, and that by changing them, we can achieve amazing things. He also learned that it takes time and practice, but the rewards are worth it. With his newfound confidence and belief in himself, Adarsh felt like nothing was impossible.

Beliefs and Neuro-linguistic programming (NLP) are closely intertwined. NLP is based on the premise that our beliefs shape our reality, and therefore changing our beliefs can enable us to create the reality we want. Our beliefs are formed through various means, such as past experiences, social and cultural conditioning, and personal values.

Through NLP techniques, individuals can identify unhelpful and limiting beliefs that they hold and challenge them. These beliefs may be hindering their personal growth or preventing them from achieving their goals. NLP techniques such as reframing, modeling, and anchoring can help individuals create a new perspective on the situation that challenges their limiting beliefs and helps them adopt a more positive and empowering belief system.

By changing beliefs, individuals can create new neural pathways in their brain, which facilitate new habits, behaviors, and attitudes. This can lead to improved self-esteem, better relationships, and greater success in life. NLP can be a powerful tool for transformative change, enabling individuals to create a personal reality that is more in line with their desired outcomes.

5. Neuroplasticity

NLP emphasizes neuroplasticity, the brain's ability to reorganize itself by forming new neural connections, which can help individuals create positive changes. The brain can be rewired through the repetition of new behaviors, thoughts and emotions.

Kirti had always felt stuck in her life. She had a lot of negative self-talk and believed that she was not capable of achieving her goals. She often found herself feeling overwhelmed, anxious, and discouraged. Despite numerous attempts to change her mindset, Kirti just couldn't seem to make any progress.

One day, Kirti's friend recommended that she try Neuro-linguistic Programming (NLP). The idea of changing her thought patterns and behavior seemed daunting at first, but she decided to give it a try.

With the help of her NLP coach, Kirti learned about neuroplasticity. She was amazed to discover that our brains have the power to change and adapt, even as adults. The coach explained that the brain is like a muscle, and just like any muscle, it can be trained and strengthened.

Kirti started practicing mindfulness meditation and visualization techniques, and she began to notice a significant improvement in her mood and overall attitude. She also learned to recognize her negative patterns of thinking, and used various NLP techniques to reframe her thoughts and reprogram her brain.

In just a few months, Kirti felt like a new person. Her confidence had grown, her anxiety had decreased, and she had a more positive outlook on life. She found herself taking on new challenges and achieving things she never thought possible. The changes were not just on the surface level, as Kirti's brain was rewiring itself thanks to neuroplasticity.

One day, Kirti reflected on her journey and was amazed at how far she had come. The power of neuroplasticity and NLP had truly transformed her life. She realized that our brains are capable of amazing things, and that by changing our thoughts and behaviors, we have the power to shape our lives.

Kirti's story illustrates the incredible potential of neuroplasticity and NLP. With the right tools and techniques, we can transform our brains and our lives. We don't have to be stuck in negative patterns of thinking or behavior, and we can always learn and grow, no matter our age or past experiences.

Neuroplasticity refers to the brain's ability to change and adapt, even in adulthood. Neuro-linguistic programming (NLP) can facilitate neuroplasticity by rewiring our neural pathways and creating new neural connections.

NLP techniques such as visualization, anchoring, and reframing can help individuals harness the power of neuroplasticity.

Visualization can stimulate the brain's motor and sensory areas, improving the efficiency of neural networks involved in the mental representation of specific movements or tasks.

Anchoring can help individuals anchor positive emotions to a particular stimulus, enhancing neural associations and reinforcing positive patterns of thought and behavior. Reframing can enable individuals to shift their perspective and create new neural pathways that are more aligned with their desired outcomes.

By using NLP to promote neuroplasticity, individuals can create lasting change in their attitudes, behaviors, and habits. Over time, these changes can become ingrained in the brain's neural networks, leading to sustained improvements in cognitive abilities, emotional regulation, creativity, and productivity.

In summary, NLP can be a powerful tool for promoting neuroplasticity, allowing individuals to rewire their brains and create lasting changes in their thoughts, behaviors, and emotions.

In conclusion, NLP helps individuals understand their mind by helping them recognize and change limiting beliefs, develop more effective communication, and improve overall mental health by connecting mind and body. With NLP techniques, individuals can create positive changes and achieve greater personal and professional success.

Chapter 3

NLP Techniques

Nathan had always struggled with public speaking. He found himself getting nervous, stuttering, and forgetting his lines every time he had to present in front of a group. This fear of public speaking was holding him back in his professional life, as he had to attend regular meetings and give presentations in his job.

One day, Nathan came across an article about Neuro-linguistic Programming (NLP) and its ability to help individuals overcome their fears and anxieties. Intrigued, he decided to look into it further.

After some research, Nathan found a qualified NLP coach who helped him understand his thought patterns and reactions when it came to public speaking. Nathan learned that his negative self-talk and limiting beliefs were holding him back. With guidance from his coach, Nathan began to implement NLP techniques to reframe his thoughts and retrain his brain.

Through the use of visualization, meditation, and other NLP tools, Nathan began to feel more confident and at ease when speaking in front of others. He was able to recognize and overcome his negative self-talk and limiting beliefs. Nathan also learned how to use language in a positive, supportive way, which helped him to remain calm and focused during presentations.

As Nathan's confidence grew, he noticed a significant improvement in his professional life. He was no longer afraid of speaking in front of groups and began to take on more challenging tasks at work. Nathan's colleagues and superiors were also impressed by his newfound confidence and skills.

Looking back, Nathan was amazed at the positive impact that NLP had on his life. Applying NLP techniques had allowed him to overcome his fear of public speaking and helped him to become a more confident person overall. Nathan realized that the benefits of NLP tools and techniques could be applied to any aspect of life, from personal relationships to professional success. It was truly life-changing, and Nathan was grateful that he had discovered it when he did.

Anchoring is a technique in Neuro Linguistic Programming (NLP) that involves associating a specific trigger or stimulus with a desired emotional or behavioral response. This can be a useful tool for managing emotions, overcoming limiting beliefs and habits, and enhancing performance in various settings.

The basic principle of anchoring is to create a sensory experience that is associated with a specific desired state or outcome. This can be done by focusing on a particular inciting event or moment, and then anchoring that experience to a specific sensory cue or trigger. Common sensory anchors include touch, sight, sound, and smell.

For example, a person struggling with public speaking may identify a specific time when they felt confident and successful while presenting. They could then anchor that experience to a particular gesture, such as touching their thumb and forefinger together.

When preparing for future speaking engagements, they could then use that gesture as a trigger to evoke the confident, successful state associated with their previous experience.

Anchoring in NLP can be a powerful tool, as it allows individuals to access positive emotional experiences and states quickly and easily. By conditioning the brain to respond to a specific trigger or stimulus in a particular way, individuals can learn to control their emotional and behavioral responses and achieve their desired outcomes.

However, it's important to note that anchoring should be used carefully and ethically. It's crucial to ensure that the anchor is a positive one and that it's being used to achieve a desirable outcome. Misusing anchoring techniques could lead to unintended negative consequences.

Here are some of the significant techniques used in NLP:

1. Anchoring

The process of creating a specific sensory trigger (such as a touch, sound or smell) to recall a positive emotion or memory.

2. Reframing

The practice of changing the way a person views a situation in order to remove negative thoughts and emotions.

Reframing is a technique used in Neuro Linguistic Programming (NLP) that involves changing the way a person views a situation or experience in order to create a more positive or useful interpretation. This can be a powerful tool for overcoming limiting beliefs, managing emotions, and promoting personal growth.

The basic premise of reframing is that the way a person interprets a situation determines how they react to it. By changing the interpretation, they can change their emotional response and behavioral reaction.

There are several types of reframing techniques used in NLP, including context reframing, content reframing, and six step reframing.

Context reframing involves changing the context in which a particular behavior or experience occurs. For example, a person struggling with a fear of public speaking might reframe their fear by viewing each speaking opportunity as an opportunity to connect with and inspire their audience.

Content reframing involves changing the meaning of a particular experience or behavior. For example, a person struggling with a fear of failure might reframe their fear by viewing each failure as a learning opportunity that will ultimately lead to their success.

Six step reframing is a more structured technique that involves identifying and resolving internal conflicts and negative emotions associated with a particular situation.

Reframing in NLP can be a powerful tool for promoting personal growth and development, as it allows individuals to shift their perspective and view challenges and experiences in a more positive and productive light.

3. Rapport

Building a positive and comfortable relationship with someone by mirroring their verbal and non-verbal cues.

Rapport refers to the sense of connection or harmony that exists between two or more people. It is a crucial component of effective communication, and is essential for building trust, establishing relationships, and achieving successful outcomes in various areas of life.

Neuro-linguistic programming (NLP) is a methodology that focuses on the language and behavior patterns that people use to achieve specific outcomes. It is based on the idea that people can change their responses and behaviors by changing the way they think and talk about their experiences.

Rapport plays a significant role in NLP, as it enables practitioners to establish a sense of trust and understanding with their clients or patients. This allows NLP practitioners to effectively communicate and influence their clients' thought patterns and behaviors, leading to positive change and personal growth.

Some techniques used in NLP to establish rapport include mirroring and matching, where individuals unconsciously mimic each other's body language, tone of voice, and communication style, and other techniques such as pacing and leading. These techniques help create a sense of mutual understanding and empathy between individuals, which facilitates more genuine communication and collaboration.

In conclusion, rapport and neuro-linguistic programming are interconnected concepts that emphasize the importance of communication, empathy, and understanding in achieving successful outcomes and personal growth. By using NLP techniques to establish rapport with others, individuals can improve their communication skills and build stronger relationships in various areas of life.

4. Submodalities

The use of sensory distinctions (such as size, color and brightness) to change the way a person experiences a thought, memory or emotion.

Submodalities in Neuro-linguistic programming (NLP) refer to the specific sensory components of a person's subjective experience. They are the building blocks that make up our mental representations of reality, and they can influence our thoughts, emotions, and behavior.

Submodalities include the qualities that we experience through our five senses, such as color, shape, size, texture, volume, distance, brightness, and movement. They can also refer to the internal processes that occur within our minds, such as the speed of our internal dialogue or the vividness of our mental images.

NLP practitioners use submodalities to help individuals change their perceptions and experiences of reality. By altering the submodalities associated with a particular experience, NLP practitioners can change the meaning and emotional response that a person associates with it.

For example, someone suffering from a fear of public speaking may have associated negative submodalities with the experience such as a blurry image of an audience and a feeling of tightness in the chest, and a frantic internal dialogue full of self-doubt. An NLP practitioner would work with the individual to identify these submodalities and then help them to replace these negative associations with positive ones, such as seeing a clear and supportive audience or feeling calm and confident when speaking; thus, changing the internal dialogue to one of peace, rather than self-doubt.

In conclusion, submodalities are an essential component of NLP, and practitioners use them to help individuals change their perceptions and experiences of reality to achieve their goals and overcome limitations. By identifying and working with a person's submodalities, NLP practitioners can create effective and long-lasting changes in behavior, thoughts, and emotions.

5. Swish pattern

A technique used to replace or interrupt a negative thought or behavior with a positive one.

The Swish Pattern is a popular technique in Neuro-linguistic programming (NLP) used to help individuals change negative thought patterns into more positive ones. The Swish Pattern is based on the idea that people think in pictures, and that the images we hold in our minds can greatly influence our thoughts, emotions, and behaviors.

The Swish Pattern technique involves two mental images - the "cue image" (or the negative image that triggers a negative thought or behavior) and the "outcome image" (or the positive image that represents the desired behavior or thought). The Swish Pattern technique works by interrupting the negative thought pattern and replacing it with the desired positive thought pattern.

The technique involves the following steps:

- Identify the negative thought pattern and its associated cue image.

- Decide on the outcome/positive image that represents the desired behavior or thought.

- See the cue image in your mind.

- Quickly bring the desired outcome/positive image into your mind in a way that overshadows the cue image.

- Make the positive image bigger, brighter, and more vivid. Then, using a "swish" gesture, imagine the cue image being replaced by the positive image.

- Repeat this process several times, gradually speeding up the process to the point where the positive image automatically replaces the cue image.

By consistently practicing the Swish Pattern technique, individuals can retrain their minds to automatically replace negative thought patterns with more positive ones, leading to improved emotional well-being and behavior.

6. Timeline therapy

The use of visual imagery and suggestion to adjust a person's perception of past events, and improve their future outlook.

Timeline therapy is a therapeutic approach that is often used in conjunction with Neuro-linguistic Programming (NLP). Timeline therapy involves working with a person's internal representation of time to help them change negative emotions, beliefs, or behaviors that are linked to past experiences.

In Timeline therapy, the therapist helps the client to access specific memories from their past and identify the limiting beliefs or negative emotions associated with those memories.

Through various techniques, the client is then guided to "recode" those memories so that they are no longer linked to negative emotions or limiting beliefs. The client is then guided to reconnect with the positive feelings and beliefs associated with those experiences.

NLP techniques are often used in conjunction with Timeline therapy to help clients achieve their desired outcomes more quickly and effectively. For example, NLP techniques such as reframing, pattern interruption, and anchoring can help clients to break free from negative patterns of thinking and behavior.

Through Timeline therapy and NLP, individuals can gain greater control over their emotions and behaviors, overcome limiting beliefs, and create more positive and empowering beliefs and behaviors for the future. By using these techniques, individuals can achieve greater success and fulfillment in all areas of their lives.

7. Meta-model

A set of linguistic tools designed to identify and challenge the limiting beliefs and assumptions a person may have.

The Meta Model is a linguistic tool used in Neuro-linguistic Programming (NLP) to help people effectively communicate and clarify their thoughts and ideas. It is a set of language patterns designed to challenge and expand people's thinking in order to uncover underlying assumptions and beliefs.

The Meta Model helps people to identify and challenge generalizations, distortions, and deletions in language, which can often lead to misunderstandings and ineffective communication. By using specific questioning techniques, this model helps to uncover more specific and precise information, providing a richer understanding of the communication.

In NLP, the Meta Model is used to identify the underlying structure of a person's language and thought patterns and to help them make changes that lead to more positive outcomes. By understanding and challenging limiting language patterns, clients can expand their thinking and develop more empowering beliefs and behaviors.

Some common Meta Model patterns include:

- **Mind Reading:** Assuming that you know what others are thinking or feeling without actually asking.

- **Lack of Referential Index:** Using pronouns (like "it", "they", or "them") without specifying what they refer to.

- **Nominalizations:** Turning verbs (actions) into nouns (things) which can create ambiguity and limit understanding of the actual action.

NLP practitioners can use the Meta Model to help people develop more accurate and effective communication skills, improve their decision-making abilities, and achieve more meaningful results in their personal and professional lives.

8. Milton model

A set of linguistic tools designed to access and influence the unconscious mind.

The Milton Model is a set of language patterns and techniques developed by Dr. Milton Erickson, a well-known psychiatrist and hypnotherapist. The Milton Model borrows heavily from Erickson's work in hypnosis and is used to communicate more effectively with people and get them to change their behaviors.

Neuro-Linguistic Programming (NLP) is a set of techniques and models for personal development and communication. It is based on the idea that language and behavior are interconnected and that by changing the way we use language, we can change our behavior and thought patterns.

NLP uses the Milton Model extensively as a tool for communication and change. The NLP practitioner uses the language patterns from the Milton Model to bypass the conscious mind and speak directly to the unconscious. This can lead to deep and immediate changes in behavior and can help people overcome limiting beliefs and patterns.

9. Parts integration

The practice of reconciling conflicting beliefs or emotions in the mind to create a more positive and unified self.

Parts Integration is a technique used in Neuro-Linguistic Programming (NLP) to help individuals integrate conflicting aspects of themselves. The technique recognizes that there may be parts within an individual that have conflicting beliefs, values, or desires, and that these conflicts may cause internal struggles or limitations.

The NLP practitioner will help the individual identify and externalize these parts, often using creative visualization or guided imagery. Then, the practitioner will use language patterns and techniques to help the parts communicate with each other, find common ground, and integrate into a more functional whole.

This technique can be used to help individuals overcome inner conflicts, make decisions, and achieve personal growth. It is often used in therapy, coaching, and personal development settings. Parts Integration is just one of the many techniques that make up the rich body of tools that NLP has to offer.

10. Hypnosis

The use of suggestion and relaxation techniques to stimulate the subconscious mind and create positive changes in behavior and outlook.

Hypnosis and Neuro-Linguistic Programming (NLP) are both modalities that focus on the power of language and communication to achieve change in people's behaviors and beliefs.

Hypnosis is a state of consciousness that can be induced through focused attention, relaxation, and suggestion. Hypnotherapists use hypnosis to help clients access their subconscious mind and suggest positive changes in their thoughts, feelings, and behaviors.

NLP, on the other hand, focuses on how we use language and nonverbal communication to create our experience of the world. NLP practitioners help clients identify and change limiting patterns of thought and behavior through language and communication techniques such as reframing, anchoring, and modeling.

Both hypnosis and NLP are often used in therapy, coaching, and personal development settings, as they allow individuals to access their inner resources and make positive changes in their lives. In fact, some practitioners use a combination of both modalities, using hypnosis to help clients access their subconscious mind and NLP techniques to help them make positive changes in their conscious thoughts and behaviors.

Chapter 4

Applications Of NLP

Neuro-Linguistic Programming (NLP) has been widely used in many fields, including personal development, counseling and therapy, coaching, communication, education, and business. Here are some of the applications of NLP:

1. Personal Development

NLP techniques are used to help individuals discover their hidden talents, overcome limiting beliefs, and improve overall mental health. It can help people gain confidence, focus, and motivation, which can lead to success in personal and professional life.

Neuro-linguistic programming (NLP) can be a powerful tool for personal development. NLP techniques can help individuals overcome limiting beliefs, negative thought patterns, and destructive behaviors. Here are some ways in which NLP can aid in personal development:

- **Setting and Achieving Goals:** NLP helps individuals to define their goals and develop strategies for achieving them. NLP techniques can help individuals to visualize their goals, break them down into manageable steps, and develop the motivation and confidence to achieve them.

- **Overcoming Limiting Beliefs:** NLP can help individuals to identify and overcome limiting beliefs that hold them back and prevent them from achieving their full potential.

- **Improving Communication Skills:** NLP can help individuals to improve their communication skills by teaching them how to read and interpret nonverbal communication, build rapport, and use language effectively.

- **Managing Emotions:** NLP can help individuals to manage their emotions by teaching them how to identify and change negative thought patterns, reframe negative experiences, and use techniques such as visualization and anchoring to create positive emotional states.

- **Enhancing Self-Awareness:** NLP can help individuals to develop greater self-awareness by teaching them to recognize and understand their own patterns of thought and behavior.

- **Increasing Self-Confidence:** NLP can help individuals to increase their self-confidence by teaching them techniques such as visualizing success, modeling successful behavior, and developing positive self-talk.

Overall, NLP can be a powerful tool for personal development. By helping individuals to overcome limiting beliefs, negative thought patterns, and destructive behaviors, NLP can help them to achieve their full potential and live a more fulfilling life.

2. Counseling and Therapy

NLP provides techniques that can help individuals deal with a range of issues like depression, anxiety, stress, and phobias. NLP techniques like anchoring, reframing, and modeling can help individuals manage their emotions and change their behavior patterns.

Neuro-linguistic programming (NLP) can be used as a complementary approach in counseling and therapy to help individuals overcome various challenges and achieve their goals. NLP techniques can be used to enhance the therapeutic process and address a wide range of issues.

Here are some ways in which NLP can be used in counselling and therapy:

1. **Increasing Self-Awareness:** NLP techniques can be used to help clients become more self-aware by identifying their thought patterns, beliefs, and behaviors that contribute to their challenges or problems.

2. **Challenging Limiting Beliefs:** NLP techniques can be used to challenge and reframe limiting beliefs held by clients that are blocking their progress in therapy.

3. **Coping with Emotions:** NLP techniques can be used to help clients manage their emotions effectively. For example, visualization techniques and anchoring can help clients shift from negative emotions to more positive ones.

4. **Developing Communication Skills:** NLP techniques can be used to help clients improve their communication skills by teaching them how to read and interpret nonverbal communication, use language effectively, and build rapport.

5. **Addressing Phobias and Trauma:** NLP techniques can be used to help clients overcome phobias and trauma by using techniques such as timeline therapy, which allows clients to revisit past experiences and change their response to traumatic events.

6. **Setting and Achieving Goals:** NLP techniques can be used to help clients set and achieve their goals by teaching them how to visualize success, break down their goals into smaller, manageable steps, and develop the motivation and confidence to achieve them.

Overall, NLP can be a useful tool in the therapeutic setting. By helping clients to develop self-awareness, challenge limiting beliefs, manage their emotions, improve their communication skills, and achieve their goals, NLP can help individuals to overcome their challenges and reach their full potential.

3. Coaching

NLP can be used to help people develop effective communication skills, manage their emotions, and become better problem-solvers. With the help of a coach, NLP-based techniques can be used to achieve specific goals in their personal and professional life.

Neuro-linguistic programming (NLP) techniques can be used in coaching to help individuals achieve their goals, enhance their performance, and improve their overall quality of life. NLP coaching is an effective way to address a wide range of issues and challenges, and can be used in both personal and professional settings.

Here are some ways in which NLP can be used in coaching:

1. **Goal Setting:** NLP techniques can be used to help clients set achievable goals by teaching them how to create clear and compelling visions of their desired outcomes, create plans of action, and develop the motivation and resourcefulness to achieve them.

2. **Overcoming Limiting Behavior Patterns:** NLP techniques can be used to help clients identify and overcome limiting behavior patterns that are holding them back from achieving their goals or full potential.

3. **Enhancing Communication Skills:** NLP techniques can be used to help clients improve their communication skills, including how to effectively communicate with others, listen actively, and build rapport.

4. **Managing Stress and Anxiety:** NLP techniques can be used to help clients manage their stress and anxiety by using techniques such as relaxation, anchoring, and visualization.

5. **Improving Performance:** NLP techniques can be used to help clients enhance their performance in various areas, such as sports, academics, or business, by teaching them how to develop better concentration, focus, and confidence.

6. **Increasing Self-awareness:** NLP techniques can be used to help clients become more self-aware by identifying their thought patterns, beliefs, and behaviors that contribute to their challenges or problems.

Overall, NLP coaching can be a powerful tool for personal and professional development. By helping individuals to set achievable goals, overcome limiting behavior patterns, enhance their communication skills, manage stress and anxiety, improve their performance, and increase their self-awareness, NLP coaching can help individuals achieve their goals, reach their full potential, and lead more fulfilling lives.

4. Communication

NLP techniques can improve communication skills by enabling people to read and respond to non-verbal cues, create rapport with others, and develop more effective listening skills.

Neuro-linguistic programming (NLP) is a technique that can be used to improve communication skills and achieve success in personal and professional relationships. It involves the following steps:

- **Rapport Building:** Establishing rapport or a connection with the person you are communicating with is essential for effective communication. It involves matching the breathing rate, tone, and body language of the person you are speaking with.

- **Body Language:** Non-verbal communication such as body language and gestures play a crucial role in communication. You can use NLP techniques to improve your body language by paying attention to your posture, eye contact, and facial expressions.

- **Language Patterns:** NLP focuses on the language patterns people use to express themselves. You can use NLP to identify the language patterns and match them during communication. This helps to create a relationship of trust and understanding.

- **Reframing:** Reframing refers to changing the context or meaning of a message to make it more positive. This technique can help you to reframe negative thoughts or beliefs into positive ones, which can improve your communication skills.

- **Anchoring:** Anchoring involves creating a physical or mental stimulus that is linked to a specific feeling or behavior. You can use NLP to create positive anchors for yourself or others that can help to improve communication.

Overall, using NLP in communication can help you to become more aware of your language, behavior, and emotions, and to communicate more effectively with others.

5. Education

NLP techniques can be used in education to improve learning and retention by teaching students how to use their senses and imagination to create associations and remember information better.

Neuro-linguistic programming (NLP) is a set of techniques that can be used to improve teaching and learning in education. Here are some ways that NLP can be used in education:

- **Goal setting:** NLP techniques can be used to help students set achievable goals and overcome obstacles that may be preventing them from achieving their full potential.

- **Creating meaningful and engaging learning experiences:** NLP encourages teachers to use language and activities that match the learning styles and preferences of their students, creating more meaningful and engaging learning experiences.

- **Improved communication:** NLP techniques can be used to teach students how to communicate more effectively with peers and teachers, improving their ability to work collaboratively and participate positively in class.

- **Enhancing memory and concentration:** NLP techniques can be used to help students improve their memory and concentration, enabling them to better recall important information and focus on key tasks.

- **Reducing stress and anxiety:** NLP techniques can be used to help students manage stress and anxiety, promoting a more positive and calm learning environment.

Overall, NLP can be a valuable tool for educators seeking to create a positive and effective learning environment. By helping students to set goals, communicate effectively, and improve their memory and concentration, NLP can empower students to achieve their full potential in education.

6. Business

NLP techniques can be used in the business world to improve leadership, time management, and decision making. It can teach sales professionals how to create rapport with customers, negotiate better, and close deals.

Neuro-linguistic programming (NLP) can be a powerful tool for business professionals to enhance their communication, influence, and leadership skills. Here are some ways that NLP can be applied in a business context:

- **Building rapport:** NLP techniques can be used to build rapport with clients, colleagues, and employees by matching their communication style, body language, and tone of voice.

- **Effective communication:** NLP helps business professionals to communicate more effectively by understanding the different communication styles of their audience and adjusting their communication style to match.

- **Goal setting and achievement:** NLP techniques can be used to set clear, achievable goals and to overcome obstacles or limiting beliefs that may be preventing individuals from achieving their goals.

- **Leadership skills:** NLP can help business leaders to develop their leadership skills by improving their emotional intelligence, understanding their team members' communication styles and motivations, and empowering team members to achieve their full potential.

- **Overcoming objections:** NLP helps business professionals to understand the underlying reasons for objections or resistance from clients, colleagues, or employees and to respond in a way that addresses their concerns and motivates them to take action.

Overall, NLP techniques can be a valuable tool for business professionals to improve their communication, leadership, and influence skills, leading to more effective collaboration, better business relationships, and increased success.

Neuro-linguistic programming (NLP) can be a powerful tool for sales professionals to influence and persuade clients in order to close deals. Here are some ways that NLP can be applied in a sales context:

- **Building rapport:** NLP techniques can be used to establish trust and build rapport with clients by matching their communication style, body language, and tone of voice.

- **Understanding client needs:** By using NLP techniques to listen carefully and ask strategic questions, sales professionals can gain a deep understanding of their clients' needs and motivations, allowing them to tailor their sales approach accordingly.

- **Using persuasive language:** NLP can be used to identify and use language patterns that are particularly impactful or persuasive for a given client or situation.

- **Overcoming objections:** By using NLP techniques to understand the underlying reasons for client objections, sales professionals can respond in a way that sincerely addresses their concerns while still persuasively making the case for their product or service.

- **Closing the deal:** NLP can be used to guide clients through the decision-making process by understanding their thought patterns and using language that motivates them to take action.

Overall, NLP techniques can be a key part of a successful sales strategy, helping sales professionals to build strong relationships with clients, uncover their needs and preferences, and persuade them to take action.

In conclusion, NLP is widely used in various fields to help individuals improve their personal and professional life. By applying NLP-based techniques, people can develop better communication skills, manage emotions more effectively, and achieve their goals.

Chapter 5

Conclusion

Key Concepts of NLP

1. **Perception is Relative:** NLP recognizes that our perception of the world is subjective and changes based on how we perceive it.

2. **The Map is not the Territory:** NLP assumes that our perception of the world is incomplete and that everyone has a unique understanding of the world.

3. **Mind and Body are Connected:** NLP views the mind and body as one system, where changes in one can lead to changes in the other.

4. **People have the Resources They Need:** NLP acknowledges that people possess the resources they need to achieve their goals, but they may need to learn how to access them.

5. **People Respond to their Experience:** NLP acknowledges that people act based on their experiences and that positive experiences can lead to positive behavior.

Roadmap for Beginners

1. Start with a Beginner's Book: The first step in learning NLP is to read a beginner's book about the subject. Examples include "NLP: The Essential Guide," by Tom Hoobyar, and "An Introduction to NLP," by Joseph O'Connor.

2. **Attend an NLP Course or Workshop:** Attend a training course or workshop to get hands-on experience with NLP techniques and concepts.

3. **Practice NLP Techniques:** Practice NLP techniques on yourself or with friends and family. Start with simple techniques such as anchoring or reframing.

4. **Learn from Experienced Practitioners:** Seek out experienced NLP practitioners to learn from them and gain insight into how they apply the techniques.

5. **Join an NLP Community:** Join an NLP community online or in person to connect with others who are interested in NLP and exchange information and ideas.

6. **Continue Learning and Practicing:** NLP is a lifelong learning journey, and it's important to continue learning and practicing new techniques to improve your skills and expand your capabilities. Attend advanced training courses, read more books, and continue to practice NLP techniques.

30 potential benefits of Neuro-Linguistic Programming (NLP) that individuals may experience:

1. Improved self-confidence and self-esteem

2. Effective communication and interpersonal skills

3. More positive thought patterns

4. Improved goal setting and achievement

5. Better stress management

6. Overcoming limiting beliefs and barriers

7. Improved decision-making skills

8. Enhanced creativity and problem-solving abilities

9. Better time management and prioritization

10. Increased motivation to achieve desired outcomes

11. More successful personal relationships

12. Improved public speaking skills

13. Greater emotional intelligence

14. Improved leadership and management skills

15. Better control over emotions and reactions

16. Overcoming phobias and fears

17. Improved emotional healing after trauma

18. Increased enthusiasm and energy

19. Enhancing sales and negotiation skills

20. Effective conflict resolution

21. Improved athletic performance

22. Enhancing academic performance

23. Reducing or eliminating procrastination

24. Greater self-awareness and mind-body connection

25. Improved memory and retention of information

26. Improved focus and concentration

27. Enhanced self-image and self-love

28. Improved sleep and relaxation

29. Overcoming addictive behaviors

30. Greater compassion and empathy for others

Success Stories with NLP

1. **Diya:** Diya had a fear of public speaking that was holding her back in her career. She tried different techniques, but nothing seemed to help. After receiving NLP coaching, Diya was able to overcome her fear and become a confident public speaker, leading to several job promotions.

2. **Daksh:** Daksh had a lack of motivation and lacked direction in his life. After receiving NLP coaching, he gained a greater sense of clarity and purpose, leading him to start his own successful business.

3. **Krupa:** Krupa suffered from anxiety and stress. After NLP coaching, she was able to manage her emotions and handle stress more effectively, leading to a happier and healthier life.

4. **Adi:** Adi had issues with self-esteem and was struggling in his personal relationships. NLP coaching helped him to overcome his limiting beliefs and improve his communication skills, leading him to build more meaningful relationships.

5. **Dipti:** Dipti had a fear of failure that was holding her back in her career. NLP coaching helped her to reframe her mindset about failure and take calculated risks, leading her to new opportunities and success.

6. **Manav:** Manav had difficulty finding common ground with his team at work. After NLP coaching, he was able to understand different communication styles and build better relationships with his colleagues, leading to a more collaborative and successful team.

7. **Rama:** Rama had issues with focus and productivity. NLP coaching helped her to identify and overcome distractions, leading her to become more productive and effective in her work.

8. **Dhiraj:** Dhiraj had difficulty maintaining healthy habits and making positive changes in his life. After NLP coaching, he was able to overcome his mental barriers and implement new habits that led to a healthier and happier lifestyle.

9. **Mouna:** Mouna had trouble making decisions, leading to indecisiveness and anxiety. NLP coaching helped her to identify her values and make confident decisions, leading to a more fulfilling life.

10. **Prasad:** Prasad struggled with anger management and lashing out in his personal and professional relationships. NLP coaching helped him to identify and manage his emotions, leading him to build stronger and more positive relationships.

50 Hacks to use NLP Techniques

1. **The Mirroring Technique:** Mirroring the body language and speech patterns of the person you are communicating with to create rapport. For example, if the person you are talking to is sitting with crossed legs, you can subtly cross your legs as well to establish a connection and make them feel more comfortable.

2. **Framing:** Using subtle language patterns to influence someone's perception of a situation. For instance, instead of saying "This will be difficult," you can reframe it as "This is a great opportunity for growth."

3. **Anchoring:** Associating a specific gesture, touch, or word with a particular emotion to trigger that emotion in future situations. For example, if you squeeze your thumb and middle finger together every time you feel confident, you can anchor that feeling of confidence and use it whenever you need a boost.

4. **Mirroring Voice Tone:** Matching the tone and pace of the other person's voice to create a deeper connection. If the person you are speaking with talks slowly and softly, try doing the same to build rapport.

5. **Embedded Commands:** Embedding subconscious directives within normal conversation. For instance, saying, "As you relax and take in this information, you'll find it easier to make a decision."

6. **Utilizing Eye Accessing Cues:** Observing a person's eye movements to gain insight into how they are processing information. If someone looks up to the left, they may be accessing their visual memories.

7. **Linguistic Presuppositions:** Using language that presupposes certain beliefs or actions. For example, asking "When you solve this problem…" instead of "If you solve this problem…"

8. **Sensory Rich Language:** Incorporating sensory words to make your message more vivid and persuasive. Instead of saying "You'll enjoy the sunshine," say "You'll feel the warm rays of the sun on your skin."

9. **Rapport Techniques:** Building rapport through body language, speech patterns, and shared experiences. You can say, "Oh, I love skydiving too! That feeling of excitement and freedom is unbeatable!"

10. **Meta Model Questions:** Challenging and expanding limited belief systems by asking questions. "How specifically do you know that's not possible?" can encourage the person to reevaluate their assumptions.

11. **Pattern Interrupts:** Breaking a person's habitual thought process to redirect their attention. Techniques include sudden movements, a change in tone, or asking an unexpected question.

12. **The Swish Pattern:** Using visualization techniques to transform negative thought patterns into positive ones. Visualize an undesirable habit and then "swish" it away with a vivid image of the desired behavior.

13. **Embedded Stories:** Sharing stories that contain embedded messages or lessons to influence behavior or belief systems. For example, sharing the story of a successful person who overcame obstacles to inspire motivation and determination.

14. **Reframing Criticism:** Reframing negative feedback as constructive criticism or an opportunity for growth. For instance, saying "Thank you for pointing out areas where I can improve, I appreciate your insights."

15. **Pre-Framing:** Setting expectations before a conversation to influence the outcome. For example, by saying "Let's approach this discussion with open minds and the intention to find a win-win solution."

16. **Metaphors:** Using metaphorical language to explain complex concepts or to present viewpoints subtly. "Life is like a journey, with ups and downs, twists, and turns. Sometimes we need to take detours but eventually, we reach our destination."

17. **Pacing and Leading:** Starting by matching someone's behavior or belief and then subtly leading them toward where you want them to go. For example, saying "I understand why you feel hesitant, but let me show you how this approach can benefit you."

18. **Yes-Set:** Getting a series of "yes" responses to establish an agreement mindset. By asking a series of escalating questions, such as "Would you like to have more success? Are you interested

in personal development? Do you believe in the power of mindset?", you are more likely to receive a "yes" when asking for their commitment.

19. **Covert Hypnosis:** Using hypnotic language patterns and suggestions to communicate with the subconscious mind. This can include embedded commands, pacing and leading, analogical marking, and non-verbal hypnotic cues.

20. **The Fast Phobia Technique:** A rapid NLP intervention to help individuals overcome phobias or fears. It involves visualizing the fear-inducing situation, intensifying it, then quickly breaking the pattern by introducing a new positive association.

21. **Time Distortion:** Altering someone's perception of time to influence decision-making. For example, creating a sense of urgency by saying, "This offer is only available for the next 24 hours."

22. **The Circle of Excellence:** Creating an imaginary circle on the ground and stepping into it to access a state of peak performance. This can be useful before a presentation or an important meeting.

23. **The Six-Step Reframe:** Helping individuals resolve internal conflicts by reframing negative thoughts and finding positive intentions behind them.

24. **Double Binds:** Presenting options to people that all lead to the desired outcome, making it difficult for them to resist. "Would you prefer to pay by cash or credit card?" presupposes that they will make a purchase.

25. **Calibration:** Developing the ability to read and interpret subtle non-verbal cues to gain insight into someone's thoughts, emotions, and intentions.

26. **Outcome Frames:** Guiding someone to define their desired outcomes to motivate and empower them. For example, asking "What specifically do you want to achieve from this session?" helps them clarify their goals.

27. **The Meta-Programs Model:** Identifying and understanding someone's meta-programs (individual thought patterns) to better communicate and influence them. These include sorting for differences or similarities, internal vs. external frame of reference, and big-picture thinkers vs. detail-oriented individuals.

28. **Reframing Limiting Beliefs:** Challenging and transforming limiting beliefs by asking questions that expand possibilities. For instance, if someone believes they are terrible at public speaking, you might ask, "Who else used to feel the same way and became a great speaker?"

29. **Linguistic Bridges:** Connecting with someone's current reality to introduce new perspectives or ideas. "Given the knowledge you already have about this topic, let's explore some additional strategies."

30. **Timeline Therapy:** Using visualization techniques to help individuals overcome past traumas or limiting beliefs by altering their perception of time and revisiting the memory from a more empowered perspective.

31. **Neuro-Logical Levels:** Considering how changes in one level of experience (environment, behavior, capabilities, beliefs, identity, and purpose) may impact another. For example, enhancing someone's beliefs around their capabilities can lead to behavioral changes.

32. **Embedded Testimonials:** Incorporating positive testimonials or success stories into your communication to reinforce credibility and confidence. Sharing stories of others who have benefited from your product or service creates social proof.

33. **Parts Integration:** Resolving inner conflicts by helping individuals acknowledge and integrate conflicting parts of their personality or desires. This allows for greater alignment and decision-making.

34. **Swinging Pendulum:** Utilizing rhythmic movements or sounds to relax and entrance someone into a more receptive state, improving their willingness to engage in suggestions or change their mindset.

35. **Fractionation:** Gradually inducing and breaking a hypnotic trance state repeatedly to increase suggestibility and create deeper psychological experiences.

36. **Pattern Overlay:** Combining the characteristics of someone the person admires with yourself to create a stronger positive impression. For example, incorporating the charisma of a beloved figure when giving a presentation to enhance your own influence.

37. **Modal Operator of Necessity (Must/Mustn't):** Recognizing when individuals have rigid rules or beliefs that limit their options

or behavior. By gently challenging their "musts" and presenting alternatives, you can expand their possibilities.

38. **Sensory Enhancement:** Using NLP techniques to sharpen one's sensory acuity and create richer experiences, such as intensified taste or heightened visual perception.

39. **The Fast Phobia Model:** A technique used to help individuals overcome specific phobias or fears rapidly. By systematically desensitizing them to the feared stimulus, negative associations can be replaced.

40. **Embedded Triggers:** Introducing subtle words or gestures that trigger certain emotions or actions without the person's conscious awareness. These triggers can be used to induce positive states or influence behavior in future encounters.

41. **The Outcome Frame:** Encouraging individuals to focus on the desired outcome rather than the problem itself. A powerful question using this frame could be, "What do you want instead?"

42. **The Milton Model:** Utilizing vague language patterns and metaphors to induce a more relaxed state or encourage open-mindedness. This model was inspired by the hypnotic language patterns used by Milton H. Erickson.

43. **Sleight of Mouth:** Responding to objections or limiting beliefs with strategic language patterns that challenge and reframe the person's perspective. For instance, responding to "I can't do it" with "What specifically makes you believe you can't? Is there any evidence to the contrary?"

44. **Multiple Perspectives Technique:** Helping individuals see situations from various viewpoints to foster empathy and understanding. By considering how others perceive a situation, they can better navigate conflicts and communicate effectively.

45. **Hypnotic Language Pauses:** Pausing strategically during conversation to create anticipation or deepen someone's focus. This can make suggestions or information more impactful.

46. **Future Pacing:** Guiding individuals to vividly imagine a successful outcome in the future, making it more likely for them to take action now.

47. **Spatial Anchoring:** Associating a particular space or location with a desired emotional state or behavior. For example, creating a dedicated workspace for focused productivity or a relaxing corner for stress relief.

48. **Congruence:** Aligning your body, voice, words, and intentions to create a strong presence and build trust. When your non-verbal behavior matches your words, the message is more persuasive and credible.

49. **The Agreement Frame:** Framing suggestions or requests in a way that emphasizes shared goals or agreement. For example, "We both value teamwork, so let's work together on this project."

50. **Modelling Excellence:** Studying successful individuals and observing their behavioral patterns, beliefs, and strategies to learn from their successes. By modeling their thoughts and actions, we can adopt their mindset for our own growth and achievement.

Appendix 2

NLP Workbook

1. **Figuring out what you want from NLP**

   Activity: Designing Your Ideal Outcome

   Instructions:

   1. Find a quiet and relaxing space where you won't be disturbed.

   2. Close your eyes and take a few deep breaths, allowing your body to unwind.

   3. Think about what you want to achieve or change in your life using NLP techniques. It could be improving your communication skills, boosting self-confidence, or overcoming a fear, for example.

   4. Visualize yourself already having achieved this outcome. See the positive changes in your life and feel the emotions associated with it.

   5. Ask yourself, "What will this outcome bring me? How will it positively impact my life and the lives of those around me?"

6. Write down your ideal outcome in a clear, concise, and positive statement.

7. Take a moment to read and reflect on your statement, ensuring it aligns with your values and represents what you truly desire.

8. Whenever you feel doubt or uncertainty, refer back to this written statement, reminding yourself of your purpose and what you want to achieve through NLP.

2. **Discovering the power of your thoughts**

   Activity: Replacing Negative Self-Talk with Positive Affirmations

   Instructions:

   1. Throughout your day, pay attention to your self-talk, the inner dialogue that you have with yourself.

   2. Whenever you catch yourself thinking negative thoughts or engaging in self-criticism, pause and become aware of these thoughts.

   3. Challenge these negative thoughts by asking yourself, "Is this thought helping or hindering my growth and well-being?"

   4. Replace these negative thoughts with positive, empowering affirmations. For example, if you think, "I always mess up important tasks," replace it with, "I am capable and confident in completing any task that comes my way."

5. Write down these positive affirmations in a notebook or create a digital list.

6. Repeat these affirmations to yourself several times a day, preferably in front of a mirror, while maintaining eye contact with yourself.

7. The more frequently you practice this activity, the more your thoughts will naturally shift toward positivity and empowerment, leading to improved self-belief and motivation.

3. **Keeping track of the gems you uncover**

Activity: Building a Success Journal

Instructions:

1. Get a journal or create a digital document specifically for your NLP journey.

2. Dedicate a few minutes at the end of each day to reflect on your experiences, insights, breakthroughs, or any valuable learnings you acquired through NLP techniques.

3. Write down your reflections in the journal, focusing on specific examples and their impact on your life.

4. Include any positive changes you noticed in your thoughts, behaviors, or emotions as a result of practicing NLP.

5. Consider adding gratitude entries, acknowledging and appreciating the progress you've made so far.

6. Regularly review your success journal to remind yourself of the growth and transformations you've experienced, reinforcing your commitment to your NLP journey.

4. Making a personal commitment to your learning

Activity: Crafting a Learning Contract

Instructions:

1. Take a few moments to reflect on your dedication and commitment to your NLP learning journey.

2. Write down a personal learning contract, outlining the specific actions and attitudes you commit to adopting throughout your NLP exploration.

3. Be specific about the activities you will engage in regularly, such as attending NLP workshops, reading books, practicing techniques, or seeking guidance from a mentor.

4. Define a timeline for achieving certain milestones or mastering specific NLP skills, being realistic and allowing yourself enough time for proper understanding and implementation.

5. Clarify the benefits you anticipate from fully committing to NLP, both in terms of personal growth and its impact on your relationships, career, or overall well-being.

6. Sign your learning contract as a symbol of your commitment and hold yourself accountable to it. Display it somewhere visible as a reminder of your dedication to your NLP journey.

5. **Having fun on the journey**

Activity: NLP Olympics

Instructions:

1. Organize or participate in an NLP Olympics event, either individually or with a group of fellow NLP enthusiasts.

2. Create a series of fun challenges or games that involve applying and demonstrating NLP techniques.

3. Examples of challenges include rapport building exercises, anchoring positive emotions, reframing limiting beliefs, or using NLP language patterns in a casual conversation.

4. Set a friendly and supportive atmosphere, encouraging everyone to explore and experiment with their NLP skills.

5. Award points or certificates for successfully completing challenges or demonstrating particular NLP abilities.

6. Throughout the event, encourage participants to reflect on their experiences, share insights, and learn from one another, fostering a sense of community and growth.

7. Celebrate the accomplishments and progress made during the NLP Olympics, fostering a positive and joyful environment for everyone involved in the journey.

www.ingramcontent.com/pod-product-compliance
Lightning Source LLC
Chambersburg PA
CBHW021134130726
47988CB00003B/1296